This is a fictionalised biography describing some of the key moments (so far!) in the career of Gareth Southgate.

Some of the events described in this book are based upon the author's imagination and are probably not entirely accurate representations of what actually happened.

Tales from the Touchline
Gareth Southgate
by Harry Coninx

Published by Raven Books
An imprint of Ransom Publishing Ltd.
Unit 7, Brocklands Farm, West Meon, Hampshire GU32 1JN, UK
www.ransom.co.uk

ISBN   978 180047 611 0
First published in 2023

Copyright © 2023 Ransom Publishing Ltd.
Text copyright © 2023 Ransom Publishing Ltd.
Cover illustration by Ben Farr © 2023 Ben Farr

A CIP catalogue record of this book is available from the British Library.

All rights reserved. No part of this publication may be reproduced, stored in a retrieval system, or transmitted, in any form or by any means, electronic, mechanical, photocopying, recording or otherwise, without the prior permission of the publishers.

The rights of Harry Coninx to be identified as the author and of Ben Farr to be identified as the illustrator of this Work have been asserted by them in accordance with sections 77 and 78 of the Copyright, Design and Patents Act 1988.

TALES FROM THE TOUCHLINE

GARETH SOUTHGATE

HARRY CONINX

For Daisy

CONTENTS

		Page
1	55 Years	7
2	Travel Agent?	15
3	Title-Winner	20
4	Cup-Winner	26
5	Swallow Me Up	31
6	Time to Reflect	37
7	New Club, Another Cup	40
8	Winding Down	45
9	That Feeling	50
10	That's Football	56
11	Building the Squad	61
12	Down – and Out	66
13	Not Easy	70
14	Result	76
15	Whatever You Do, Do It Soon	82
16	Shoot-Out	88
17	Naïve	95
18	A Great Team	99
19	Semi-Finalist	103
20	Finalist	109
21	Next Stop Qatar	116

1
55 YEARS

June 2021, Wembley Stadium, London, England
Euro 2020 Round of 16, England v Germany

Fifty-five years. That's how long it had been since England had beaten Germany in a competitive knockout game. The last time was back in 1966 – also the last time England had won a major trophy.

Since then, they'd been defeated several times by their arch-rivals. There'd been heartbreak in 1970, 1990 and 2010.

And now they had to do it all over again.

"We had three at the back at the World Cup," Gareth told his coaches, as they all sat around the meeting table, discussing their options for tomorrow's game. "And Germany play with three as well. Maybe we should go toe-to-toe?"

"Is that a bit negative?" Steve Holland, his assistant, asked. "Makes us look like we're scared. We should stick with our 4-3-3, play to our strengths."

"I'm not sure," Gareth mused. "And who to play? We've got too many options."

Euro 2020 had been a long time coming, having been delayed for a year due to the coronavirus pandemic. It had been a year of planning for Gareth and his team, a year of praying for no injuries, of watching the form of his players carefully, and looking for anyone who could give England the edge at the tournament.

Three years ago, England had got all the way to the semi-finals of the World Cup, earning Gareth his reputation as one of England's best-ever managers. He knew that, even if they lost tomorrow, he would keep his job.

But he hadn't become the England manager just to keep his job. He wanted to make history. And to do that, he'd need to make the big decisions.

Gareth looked at Steve, his face beaming. When he'd first taken the job, he'd been desperate to find players. Now he had the likes of Phil Foden, Jack Grealish, Marcus Rashford and Jadon Sancho to choose from. And that was without even mentioning Bukayo Saka, who had started the final group game against Czechia, impressing everyone in the stadium and at home.

"Phil and Raheem Sterling are the favourites, surely," Steve Holland said. "Supporting Kane."

"I think we should reward good performances," Gareth said firmly. "Bukayo starts. And he works hard defensively. He's got pace, energy. He's key to our team."

He paused, looking again at Steve Holland. "We're going three at the back. Trippier comes in."

Now, as Gareth was sitting in the the dressing room, moments before the game, he looked around at his squad. Gently he rested his head in his hands and rubbed his eyes.

Last night, with his coaches, he'd been so confident.

He had been firm in his decision to go three at the back, to play Bukayo Saka alongside Raheem Sterling and Harry Kane.

But now, looking over his squad, he had Foden, Grealish, Rashford and Sancho all left on the bench. Had he made the wrong choice? He knew he had five substitutes to make changes, but the game could be done by then. But then, he'd already made his decision – he just needed the confidence to stick with it.

Gareth stood up and cleared his throat, silencing the chatter amongst his players. They all turned to look at their manager.

"Germany," he said, letting the name hang in the air. "For over fifty years, they've stopped us," he continued. "We know exactly what they've done to us, I don't need to tell you. Today we have an opportunity to make history, to put ourselves in the quarter-finals of the Euros – to take a step towards winning our first major trophy since '66."

He paused, using the drama of the moment. "We're at home, we've got the Wembley crowd behind us. We won't have a moment like this again – we have to make it count."

He knew he didn't need to say any more. If he couldn't get his players motivated for a game against Germany, then there was no hope.

The crowd at Wembley was almost totally England supporters, and they were loud, boisterous. Any other nation would have found it a very difficult place to be, but Gareth knew that the Germans were different. They wouldn't be intimidated by the atmosphere.

But it did help to inspire his players. Raheem Sterling went close, cutting inside and whipping a shot that Neuer parried behind. Then, before half-time, Harry Kane almost put England ahead, but he was tackled before he could convert his chance.

Gareth had spent most of the first half sitting in his dugout. He didn't need to run up and down to get his players going. They knew what they needed to do.

He turned to Steve Holland. "What do you think?" he asked. "Any changes?"

"It's working well," Holland said cautiously. "We've limited their chances. Bukayo has been brilliant."

Gareth nodded. So far, England had been in control of the match. Germany had had chances, with Kai

Havertz and Timo Werner both getting shots on goal. But Gareth wasn't too worried.

"Give it fifteen and then we make changes, try and go for it," Gareth said.

The second half was slower. With more at stake, both teams were nervous. Gareth could feel the anxiety building amongst the fans. They wanted a change. But Gareth was waiting for the right moment.

Then, just before the 70th minute, he stood up.

"Jack! You're coming on," he called over to Jack Grealish on the bench.

"You know what to do," Gareth told him. "Play your natural game. Dribbling, running, commit players, cause problems. You've got 20 minutes to win us the game. Go and do it."

Gareth called Bukayo Saka off when Grealish went on. Gareth felt bad at removing him, but he knew it was the right choice. Making hard decisions was part of his job.

This time, Gareth had got it right. The change made an instant impact. Grealish picked up the ball and waited for the right moment, before slipping the ball into Shaw, who got a cross in. Raheem Sterling was lurking in the box, and the City winger side-footed the ball into the back of the net.

The noise that erupted in the stadium was not something Gareth had ever heard before. It wasn't even a full crowd, but the wall of sound was still deafening.

Gareth himself was sucked in, grabbing his coaches and punching the air. He knew the game wasn't won yet, but even so, he celebrated wildly. This could be his biggest moment as England manager.

Barely a minute later, Germany burst clear and the ball was slipped into Thomas Müller, the man who had tormented England in 2010. Müller raced through, one-on-one with Pickford. Gareth could barely watch.

Müller pulled his right foot back and slid the ball towards goal. It went past Pickford and raced past the post, out of play. Müller had missed a huge chance.

The cheer that went up from the England fans was almost as loud as when they had scored.

Then, a few minutes later, England doubled their lead. Once again, it was Grealish who provided the assist. He got the ball on the left-hand side and flicked it across the box, for Kane to head home.

England 2, Germany 0 – with five minutes left.

Now Gareth allowed himself to celebrate properly. Even he believed that the game was done now. England were just five minutes from a European quarter-final.

Those five minutes felt like a week, with Gareth and his coaches watching anxiously from the sidelines.

Then, at last, the full-time whistle went. The game was over. England had won.

Gareth held his arms high, basking in the praise and celebrations of the England fans. He remembered his own personal heartbreak against Germany in 1996. He remembered the criticism of his England team just three years ago. They'd said he could only beat easy teams.

Tonight, the England players had proved them all wrong. *He'd* proved them all wrong too. He'd got the big decisions right – three at the back, Bukayo Saka in the attacking line-up.

Beating Germany was a big moment, but Gareth wasn't satisfied yet. He wanted to win the whole thing. He wanted to be the most successful England manager since 1966.

And he was going to make it happen.

2
TRAVEL AGENT?

March 1987, Crystal Palace Training Ground, Croydon, England

"Come on, Nord! Get moving!" The gruff shout from Crystal Palace's reserve team manager, Alan Smith, boomed across the car park. Gareth winced at the nickname, but didn't say anything. He picked up his bag, heaved it over his shoulder and stumbled over to the minibus, where the manager was sitting, waiting for him.

"Quick!" Smith shouted again. "We're going to be late!"

He'd been given the name Nord just after starting at Crystal Palace. The squad was full of local south Londoners, and Gareth's soft Crawley accent easily stood out.

A few of the coaches had said he sounded like Dennis Norden, a guy on the radio that Gareth had never heard of. The nickname had stuck.

It had reinforced Gareth's reputation as a softly spoken, hard-working player who was also committed to his studies at the local college.

College made sense. For all promising young players, there was a good chance that football wouldn't work out. Gareth's interest in journalism gave him a career that he would be more than happy to fall back on. But his heart really lay with football.

Despite his soft-spoken ways, on the pitch he was like a different person. He played hard, never afraid of a tackle, and was full of passion and determination. Having something to prove only increased his commitment.

He was hugely vocal on the pitch too. More often than not, he'd be wearing the captain's armband.

He was wearing it today, as he raced across the car

park to the minibus and his waiting manager. He slumped into his seat and stretched out his legs, feeling the tightness in his thighs.

They had just finished a match for the youth team, and now they were on their way to the second game of the day. Gareth wasn't the only player to be involved in both games, but he was the only player to be sure of playing every minute of both matches.

"You'll be playing for the first team on Saturdays soon as well, Gareth, mate," Smith chuckled, turning in his seat to face him.

"You think so? Do you think I can get there?" Gareth asked. He was 17 now – about the age that players started making the transition from the reserve team into the first team.

Smith shrugged. "They're watching you, mate, for sure. Don't worry, the guys know who you are."

"So, when can I make that step up?" Gareth asked.

"You've got to be patient, Nord, mate. Just focus on today's game."

Gareth sat back in his seat. This wasn't the first time that they'd had this conversation, but each time, he got the same, unsatisfying answer. Each time, he was told to focus on the game coming up.

At the ground for the second game, they got off the minibus and headed over to the small pitch. Gareth pulled up his captain's armband and gathered his team-mates.

"I know most of us have just played a match," he said, starting his little pep-talk – something he always did before a game. "But we've been doing two games a day for the last few months now. We're fitter than this team, and we know their strengths – and their weaknesses."

He looked around at his team-mates, making a mental note of those who looked tired. Gareth had always had a talent for working out how to motivate people and get them onside.

He'd played in a number of different positions in his short career at the Crystal Palace academy – centre-midfield, right-back, left-back – and centre-back, which was where he preferred to play. He could dictate the game from there, spraying passes out wide to his wingers and into his forwards. He loved getting involved in the scrap, flying into challenges, jostling and shoving with the strikers at corners.

The pitch was muddy and rain was now coming down hard. Both teams were soaked and covered in mud.

Despite their commitment, the second game of the day was too much for the Palace players, and they were soundly beaten. Even so, at the end of the game Gareth went over and shook hands with the opposition players. It was the right thing to do.

When he turned round, he saw fury on his manager's face. "This is your problem, Nord!" Smith fumed. "You're too busy worrying about the opposition! Look after us, look after yourself, not them!"

Gareth just stood there, astonished.

"You've got the skills, the communication, the intelligence," Smith went on, "but … this is why you've not got the step-up into the first team. You're good enough, but … I don't know. Sometimes I just wonder if you should go and become a travel agent or something."

Gareth felt the tears welling up in his eyes. But he couldn't cry, not here.

"Look," Smith said, softening his tone, "focus on the football, show us what you've got. It's not too late for you, kid. I still believe in you."

3
TITLE-WINNER

May 1994, Ayresome Park, Middlesbrough, England
Middlesbrough v Crystal Palace

This is why they've not given you the step-up.

Alan Smith's words raced around in Gareth's head as he stood in the players' tunnel, several hundred miles from his home. It was a warm May afternoon in the North-East, but the pitch was still muddy and wet.

Smith had uttered those words seven years ago, when Gareth had been an excitable, eager 17-year-old, desperate to get his chance. In those days he'd been naïve, not really understanding the competitive aspect of becoming a professional footballer.

Gareth nervously straightened the captain's armband that was around his right arm, looked back at his team and smiled.

Smith's words had toughened him up and, a few years later, he'd forced his way into the Crystal Palace first team. By 1992 he was a regular in the starting eleven, playing in different positions across the back four and in defensive midfield.

It hadn't quite been the route he'd planned. He'd really wanted to be a centre-back, to be the man at the heart of the defence, dominating the game from there.

But part of toughening up meant being more professional. He had to do what was right for the team, and if that meant playing in a position he didn't particularly enjoy, then he was happy to do that.

On top of that, his intelligence, his natural demeanour and his willingness to put the team first meant that he was a natural pick for captain.

Palace had been relegated from the Premier League

in their first season there, and they were now in Division One. They had a talented squad, including Chris Armstrong, Chris Coleman and John Salako. There were more talented players than Gareth in the team, and more senior players too.

But Gareth was the glue that held it all together. He wasn't intimidating or dominating – that wasn't his style. He had a quiet authority and just knew how to manage the big egos, how to get the players onside and working for the team.

Palace's aim for this season was simple – to win back promotion to the Premier League. They had a new manager this season too, in Alan Smith – the same guy who'd given Gareth such a hard time all those years ago. But now their relationship was very different.

"Nord, you're my right-hand man," Smith had told him at the start of the season. "You're my eyes and ears on the pitch. Keep the guys in line. If we keep on the right track, then we've got what it takes to get ourselves back in the Prem."

Gareth and Smith had indeed kept the players focused, kept them on the straight and narrow, lifting their spirits when the defeats had come, and getting them to raise their game at critical moments.

A couple of weeks ago, it had all paid off. Palace had sealed promotion back to the Premier League.

But today there was more at stake – the Division One title. Nottingham Forest had finished the season with a good run of form and were right behind Palace in the table. A win for Palace today, at Middlesbrough, would seal the title for them.

"Can't we just celebrate now?" Chris Armstrong moaned. "We've got promotion – that's what matters. Why bother about the title?"

"We've come all this way," Gareth answered softly. "We deserve to get our hands on a trophy, get a medal around our neck. Until that trophy is in my hands, we don't celebrate."

Armstrong grunted, but he backed down. Over the season, Gareth had earned the respect of his team-mates. He'd got them this far – they weren't going to cross him now.

The pitch was muddy and slow, with the ball often getting stuck or rolling unpredictably. It caught Gareth and his team off-guard and it allowed Middlesbrough to take an early lead.

The cheers of the 'Boro fans around them were loud and demoralising, but Gareth clapped his hands together and shouted to his team-mates.

"It's early days, guys!" he insisted. "We've got a long time to get back in this! Keep doing what we've been doing all season!"

Five minutes later, Gareth put Palace back level. A free kick was floated in and he rose high above the Middlesbrough defence, heading the ball towards the far corner.

It drifted through the air, past the outstretched arm of the keeper, and nestled in the back of the net.

"Come on!" Gareth cheered, pumping his fist.

He had popped up with a few goals this season, but this may have been his most important.

Palace were back on track and, from then on, they were as good as they'd been all season. Chris Armstrong and David Whyte added further goals, as Palace ran out 3-2 winners.

They had sealed both the Division One title and

promotion to the Prem, at the first time of asking. Next week, Gareth would be lifting the trophy – the first of his career – in front of their own fans.

Gareth was given a big hug by Alan Smith, as the coaching staff charged onto the pitch at the end of the match.

"I always knew you'd do it, Nord," he beamed. "I always knew you'd make it. 'Division One Champions!' It's got a nice ring to it."

Gareth just smiled.

His thoughts were already on the next season, in the Premier League. He'd shown that he could dominate Division One – now he wanted to mix it with the best.

He couldn't wait.

4
CUP-WINNER

March 1996, Wembley Stadium, London, England
League Cup Final, Aston Villa v Leeds

It was an insane number – one that Gareth still couldn't quite wrap his head around. Two and a half million pounds. That was how much Aston Villa had paid Crystal Palace to acquire Gareth Southgate.

Palace's first season back in the Premier League hadn't gone as well as they'd hoped. Despite finishing on a huge 48 points, the club had been one of four teams that were relegated that year, as the Premier League downsized to 20 teams.

Palace had been unlucky but, to Gareth, it didn't matter. Relegation was relegation, and he didn't want it. He'd never intended to leave Palace – it was where he'd been given his first chance at professional football and where he'd made his name. But he couldn't face another season back in the second tier of English football. He needed to be playing club football at the highest level – in the Premier League.

The manager and the chairman at Palace both understood his position and made it clear that they weren't going to stand in his way. But then Gareth heard the asking price. Two and a half million. He knew that transfer prices had been rising over the past few years, but even so – that was way too much. There was no way that anybody was going to pay that for a centre-back.

Were Palace asking such a high price so that nobody would want him? Was he looking at Division One football again next year?

Then, only a couple of weeks later, Aston Villa offered the full asking price. The deal was done quickly and Gareth was soon a Villa player – in the Prem.

After narrowly missing out on the title a couple of years ago, Villa had finished last season in 18th, only just avoiding relegation. They were managed by Brian Little, and he was now turning the side around, moving on the older players and bringing in younger, fresher legs.

Gareth was part of his plan. He was the key cog in the centre of defence, forming a dominant back three with Paul McGrath and Ugo Ehiogu.

Villa were now once again threatening the top of the Premier League table, and this increased Gareth's profile. As a result, in December, he'd got international recognition, being called up to the England squad for the first team.

There was more joy still to come. By March, Villa had reached the final of the League Cup, where they would be taking on Leeds. Villa had won this competition just two years earlier, and success in this final would put them level with Liverpool as the most successful team in the competition, with five wins.

The final was played at Wembley, on an overcast, muggy day. Even so, the pitch was in pristine condition.

As he stood on the pitch before the final, Gareth

thought about the last game he'd played for a trophy – that match in the far north of England, battling through the mud to win the Division One title for Palace. Now he was an England international, playing for one of the best clubs in the country.

He brushed the hallowed Wembley turf with his hand, feeling the smooth grass. He still couldn't really believe how things had worked out. He'd always hoped to make it as a footballer, but he hadn't anticipated being a player who'd cost millions of pounds.

"Stick tight to Yeboah," he reminded Ehiogu. "He'll want to turn you. Don't let him. And Gary," he shouted across to his right wing-back, Gary Charles, "watch the runs of Speed!"

Gareth may not have been the captain of the Villa team, but he was still a natural leader. Organising the back three just came instinctively to him. He also had a good instinct for how to get the best out of the defence. And they listened to him, trusted him.

Leeds were a good team but, this season, Villa were better. Gareth was on top form at the back, winning every aerial battle, timing every tackle to perfection.

And he was the loudest player on the pitch, constantly instructing his team-mates where to go, who to cover, motivating them, firing them up.

Savo Milošević fired Villa ahead after 20 minutes, and then further goals from Ian Taylor and Dwight Yorke sealed a glorious 3-0 League Cup win.

As Gareth climbed the Wembley steps with the rest of the Villa team, he thought about where he'd been a few years ago, struggling to get into the Palace team. More than once he'd accepted – if only very briefly – that his future was going to be in journalism instead.

But here he was, climbing the steps at England's national stadium, about to get his hands on the second trophy of his career.

He collected his medal and got his chance to lift the trophy as it was passed around. But his thoughts were already moving on.

There was a European Championships coming up this summer and he had a good chance, not just of being part of the squad, but of being in the first team.

He had fought his way to get this far in his career. Now he was looking for the next challenge.

this very pitch. Now he was part of the England team, in a penalty shoot-out against Germany.

Four years ago, a 21-year-old Gareth had sat at home with a few mates, watching the 1992 Euros in Sweden.

"Wouldn't it be great to be there in '96?" he'd said to them. "Playing for England."

They'd thought he was joking. Back then, Gareth hadn't even established himself in the Palace team, and the idea of playing for his country just seemed crazy.

But his mates had all been deceived by Gareth's quiet manner. He might have seemed quite modest, almost unassuming, but underneath it all there was a steely determination.

In any case, Gareth's career had skyrocketed in the last four years. He'd gone from making his England debut in December, to now being an integral part of the team, lining up alongside captain Tony Adams, the legendary centre-back. The dream of representing his country had taken another twist.

The Euro 96 competition was being hosted by England, so every match was being played in front of a passionate home crowd.

5
SWALLOW ME UP

June 1996, Wembley Stadium, London, England
Euro 96 Semi-Final, England v Germany

"If it goes to six, will you take one?" the England manager Terry Venables, asked Gareth, grabbing him by the arm

Gareth looked around at his team-mates. A few them were tying their laces. Some looked as though were in prayer.

How had it all come to this so suddenly? Just months ago, he'd won the League Cup, with Vil

The last time England had hosted a major tournament was 30 years ago, in 1966, when they'd gone on to win the World Cup. Needless to say, there was intense pressure on the current squad to match the heroes of '66.

After a slow start, with a 1-1 draw against Switzerland and a hard-fought 2-0 win over Scotland, England had come alive in the final group game.

Gareth had had the job of man-marking world class striker Dennis Bergkamp – and he'd totally succeeded in that task, with Bergkamp barely getting a sniff as England ran out 4-1 winners.

In the quarter-finals, England had ended their penalty shoot-out curse with a win over Spain, putting them into the semi-finals of a major tournament for the first time since 1990. And, just like in 1990, they were up against old rivals Germany.

The match was a tense affair. The England fans careered from loud and boisterous, to nervous and quiet, as the game ebbed and flowed. Shearer blasted England ahead, but then Stefan Kuntz quickly pulled the Germans level.

At the full-time whistle, it was still level.

Extra time came and went – still level.

Once more, England faced penalties.

England knew their first five penalty-takers, but after that, they hadn't made plans. Gareth wasn't amongst the first five, but he was sure that stepping forward and volunteering to take one was the right thing to do.

"If it goes to six, will you take one?" Terry Venables asked Gareth again.

Gareth nodded, gulping slightly, not sure he'd be able to get the words out if he tried to speak. Venables nodded and moved on, talking to each of the players in turn, assembling his list.

" 'You taken a pen before, Gaz?" Bryan Robson asked Gareth, spotting the concern on his face.

"Yeah," he replied.

Thankfully, Robson didn't ask for any more details. Gareth *had* taken one penalty before – for Crystal Palace, three years ago. He'd missed.

Inwardly, he prayed that it wouldn't go to six. Surely it would all be done by then.

Shearer scored first. Then Thomas Häßler equalised.

Platt scored. Strunz equalised.

Pearce, Gascoigne and Sheringham all scored. And the Germans matched them, goal-for-goal.

It was 5-5. Gareth was up next.

It was a long walk from the half-way line to the penalty spot. He'd practised taking penalties in training, but he'd forgotten about the walk. They hadn't practised that.

He needed to think about what to do, where he was going to place it. His mind was reeling as a thousand different thoughts swirled around in his head. *Focus!* he told himself.

He decided he was just going to put it in the corner. That made sense.

He placed the ball on the spot, trying not to look at the keeper or the fans chanting behind the goal. He desperately wanted to turn around now, let someone else take the penalty. But he couldn't. It was just him, the ball and the keeper.

He put the ball down and took several steps back, marching almost all the way back to the edge of the area. Was he too far away? He wasn't sure. He'd never scored a penalty before.

He charged forward and swung his right boot, aiming to his left, looking to put it in the corner. He saw the keeper dive the right way.

Then Gareth watched with horror as the huge gloved hand of Andreas Köpke met the ball, cannoning it back out towards him.

His penalty had been saved.

He trudged back to his team-mates, not daring to look them in the eye, not looking at the German penalty-taker coming the other way.

He barely even registered Andreas Möller smashing his penalty high into the back of the net, doing exactly what Gareth wished he had done.

England were out. Once again, they had lost to the Germans on penalties in a semi-final. And Gareth was the one who had missed.

He wanted the ground to swallow him up. He wanted to disappear from the sight of everyone in the stadium.

He had let the whole country down.

6
TIME TO REFLECT

May 2000, Wembley Stadium, London, England
FA Cup Final, Aston Villa v Chelsea

Wembley Stadium held a lot of memories for Gareth. It was where he'd won his first major trophy, lifting the League Cup with Aston Villa, and it was where he'd played numerous times for his country.

But it was also where he'd experienced his greatest failure – a moment, four years ago, that would haunt him for the rest of his life.

After the final, his mum had asked him, "Why didn't you just smash it?"

Over the years, he'd asked himself the same question dozens of times. He'd run through those moments so many times in his head, imagining himself putting the ball into the top corner, or dinking it down the middle. But what had happened, happened. The moment had come and gone and he – and England – were left with the consequences.

At the time, he'd thought that taking that sixth penalty was the bravest thing he could have done. It had seemed to be the right thing to do for the team. But now he could see that he'd been wrong. The bravest thing he could have done would have been to say no. He should have said he wasn't ready. At that moment, England had needed a penalty – and he hadn't been ready to deliver that.

Today, Gareth was back at Wembley, this time with Aston Villa, leading the team out in the final of the FA Cup. Four years ago, he'd marched out here with this team and won the League Cup.

But this was different. The FA Cup was a trophy that Villa hadn't won in 43 years. And today they were up against a Chelsea side who were one of the best in the country. It would not be an easy game.

It was a drab first half. Chances were few and far between, with neither side willing to open up and really go for the match.

In the second half, Chelsea began to create better chances, but it took until the 73rd minute for the deadlock to be broken. An error by Villa keeper David James allowed the ball to fall at the feet of Roberto di Matteo, who blasted it into the back of the net.

It was an uphill battle for Villa from then on, and Chelsea were resilient, composed and in control for the rest of the match. At the whistle, the FA Cup was theirs.

Once again, Gareth had suffered Wembley heartbreak – although this time at least it didn't feel as if it was all his fault.

He was 29 now, with just two trophies to his name. On top of that, he was part of a Villa side that seemed to be stuck in the same place, season after season.

Gareth knew that the end of his career wasn't too far away now. He wanted to end it in style.

He needed a new challenge.

7
NEW CLUB, ANOTHER CUP

February 2004, Millennium Stadium, Cardiff, Wales
League Cup Final, Middlesbrough v Bolton

Gareth's Aston Villa career had come to a fairly disappointing end. After the highs of lifting the League Cup trophy and reaching the final of the FA Cup, the progress Villa had made had indeed faltered.

He'd informed the Villa hierarchy of his intention to move on, and in the summer of 2001 he'd left the club for Middlesbrough, for a fee of £6.5 million.

A year later, after the departure of Paul Ince, Gareth was appointed the new captain of Middlesbrough.

Middlesbrough weren't as good a team as Villa, lacking both the history and the legacy of competing at the top of the table, but they did have a large group of passionate fans. Gareth had experienced them first-hand during his time with Villa and with Palace, and he'd never felt more appreciated than when he was playing at the Riverside Stadium.

Middlesbrough's manager was Steve McClaren, somebody who Gareth had worked with before, as part of the England squad. At 'Boro, McClaren was putting together a highly competitive team, already including the likes of Juninho, George Boateng, Gaizka Mendieta and Boudewijn Zenden.

Gareth had also been joined at Middlesbrough by his former Villa teammate Ugo Ehiogu, and they made a combative and dominant centre-back partnership.

"Normally, I'd say, let's push for a top-half finish," McClaren had told the players at the start of the season. "I'd say, let's make sure we avoid relegation, then see where it goes from there."

McClaren had paused, gauging the reaction of the team. He knew there were a number of players in the squad who were wanting more than just "dodging relegation" as a season target. He wanted to keep them on board – *and* use their expectations to raise the team's overall ambitions.

"This club hasn't won a trophy in over 100 years," he'd told them. "We have an opportunity now, more than any squad in this club's history, to win a cup, whether it's the FA Cup or the League Cup."

Gareth had taken up the mantle then. "At the end of your careers, lads," he told them, "you'll look back – and do you know what you'll be proud of?"

He paused, letting the question hang. "You won't be proud of the top-ten finishes, the 'avoiding relegations'. You'll look at your medals, the finals you've won.

"I've lost finals," he continued. "And I've won some. Whatever the result, *those* are the games I remember. So let's make sure we create some great memories."

This season, 'Boro had targeted the League Cup. It wasn't as prestigious as the FA Cup and so was slightly easier to win. Even so, it was still a major competition.

The club fought hard through the rounds, but with

focus and effort they came through two penalty shootouts and two difficult legs in the semi-finals, against an Arsenal side that would go on to be invincible in the Premier League.

They made it to the final, which set them up with a game against a tough Bolton side, managed by Big Sam Allardyce.

"We know how Bolton are going to play," Gareth told his players. "They're going to scrap and fight for every ball. We will have to fight harder."

"We get an early goal," McClaren added. "Start hard and fast, put them on the back foot. They'll struggle – we can take advantage of that."

The game started and McClaren had barely sat down in his seat before 'Boro took the lead. Bolo Zenden got down the left wing and his cross was met by Joseph-Désiré Job, who put them ahead.

A few minutes later, they had a penalty, which Zenden converted to double their lead.

Bolton struck back through Kevin Davies, and they continued to pile on the pressure, with Mark Schwarzer being forced into a number of great saves.

Ehiogu and Gareth were oustanding in defence, defending every cross and blocking every shot, as 'Boro held on for the win.

Gareth had won the League Cup for the second time in his career – with two different clubs – and once more he climbed the steps to lift the trophy.

He was the first Middlesbrough captain in over 100 years to lift a major trophy, and it cemented his place in the history of the club.

But now, aged 33, Gareth knew that his career was winding to a close. There was a good chance that this would be the last trophy of his career.

He had no idea what the future held. He'd discussed going into management with some of his coaches, but he'd thought about punditry as well.

He wasn't sure exactly what he would be doing after retirement, but he did know one thing – he wanted to continue in the game in some way.

Football had given him so much. Perhaps it would be time to give something back.

8
WINDING DOWN

May 2006, Philips Stadion, Eindhoven, The Netherlands
UEFA Cup Final, Middlesbrough v Sevilla

Middlesbrough were flying. Having won their first trophy in over 100 years, they were now regularly in the top seven of the Premier League, and for two consecutive seasons they had sealed a place in European football.

Now 35, Gareth had retired from international duty a few years ago and was now weighing up his options as his club career wound down.

"So your contract is up at the end of next season," McClaren mused, looking over the sheets in front of him. "Are you thinking of retiring, Gareth? You could probably go on for a few more years."

"I haven't really thought about it," Gareth admitted. "But, I think, probably yeah. The game's getting too fast for me, and I don't want to get in the way of the youngsters."

"We could do with you here," McClaren said. "You know – help them come through, show them the ropes. We can't keep our place in the top seven forever, so there's going to be difficult times ahead."

"You think we'll be back battling relegation?" Gareth asked. 'Boro weren't a big club – they couldn't compete with some of the big-spending teams in the Prem.

"Maybe," McClaren confessed. "We could do with experienced heads like you around, keep everyone motivated."

"I'm not sure … "

"Then what about coaching?" McClaren asked. "One more year playing with us, then maybe step up to join the coaching staff. Have you done your courses?"

"I've done some, but I've not had the time," Gareth

admitted. "Remember, I was playing international football until a couple of years ago."

"Think about getting them done," McClaren told him. "You'd be a real asset to us – I think you'd make a good manager."

Retirement might be looming, but Gareth still hadn't thought much about his future. He knew that some players had their whole careers mapped out, but he hadn't made those kinds of plans. He'd never even really imagined himself making it as a footballer.

He tried to picture himself on the sidelines, shouting instructions, making decisions, picking the team. He couldn't quite see it. He wanted to be out there on the pitch, influencing the game.

Even so, he still had another year to go. Which was fine – there were still some big games to come.

Middlesbrough had been involved in the UEFA Cup this season and, after cruising through the group stage, they had secured hard-fought wins against Stuttgart and Roma. Then came two dramatic, last-gasp comebacks against Basel and Steaua Bucharest, to set 'Boro up with a final against Sevilla.

Sevilla were a big club, with far more experience in the UEFA Cup and the Champions League. Beating them was going to be an incredibly tough ask. For 'Boro to have even got this far was an achievement in itself. But they wanted more.

Despite Gareth's age, and with talk of retirement fresh in his mind, he was still the man to lead them out for the final, the man they would look to for inspiration.

"Look, lads," he told the players, gathered around him in the dressing room. "We've come through some pretty tough matches to get here. By rights we should have been out of this competition two rounds ago. But we're here."

He looked around as the players all nodded in agreement – players he knew would fight tooth and nail for this match.

He knew they would go on to have long careers, maybe longer and more illustrious careers than his had been. But, for now, he was the man they listened to.

"No matter what happens out there, we keep fighting," he continued. "We've shown we can come back – sometimes from near-impossible positions. There's no reason we can't do it again today."

In the end, Sevilla were far too strong. If Gareth had thought that the Premier League forwards were getting too quick for him, the Sevilla strikers were on another level. Players like Luís Fabiano, Javier Saviola and Jésus Navas were close to impossible to mark. Every touch was superb, every pass lightning quick.

Sevilla opened the scoring inside 30 minutes and then added three more in the final 15 minutes of the game.

At the final whistle, Gareth slumped to the floor, exhausted. 'Boro had done so well to get this far in the tournament – an achievement in itself – but in this game they'd been thoroughly outplayed, completely thrashed.

Even so, having got so close, it stung to have lost in the final.

Gareth had been vaguely thinking about retirement at the end of next season but, as he watched the Sevilla players celebrating with the trophy, he began to think about retiring sooner. Perhaps his time at the highest level of football had come to an end.

Perhaps it was time to step into coaching.

9
THAT FEELING

August 2006, Riverside Stadium, Middlesbrough, England
Middlesbrough v Chelsea

In the end, all it took was a penalty shoot-out defeat for England – against Portugal at the World Cup – and a few phone calls.

As a result of England's World Cup performance, the England manager, Sven Göran-Eriksson, was sacked. He was replaced by Middlesbrough manager Steve McClaren. Suddenly, after years of security – and two major cup finals – Middlesbrough were looking for a new manager.

A number of candidates were approached for the role, including Terry Venables, Martin O'Neill and Alan Curbishley. Steve Gibson, the 'Boro chairman, had a clear vision for the future. He wanted to carry on McClaren's good work and push on, hopefully ending up with a place in the Champions League.

It hadn't occurred to Gareth to apply for the job. He'd secretly hoped that he might end up on the new manager's coaching staff at some point, but he didn't think he was ready for the top job yet.

But Gibson had other ideas. After a long and difficult search, Gibson's office finally put in a call to Gareth.

"Gareth, we've looked at so many people, spoken to so many managers and coaches," he told him. "But I just keep coming back to you. You're articulate, you're well-spoken, you're highly respected in the dressing room. They're all qualities a top manager needs."

"But I've not even finished all my coaching badges," Gareth replied.

"The guys here think that's fine," Gibson answered.

"We can talk to the FA, the Premier League, get a special agreement. So that's no problem. Is that your only concern?"

Gareth hesitated. Playing in the UEFA Cup final against Sevilla, he'd begun to feel quite out of his depth, and he was still thinking about quitting at the end of this coming season. Why not do it now and become manager of 'Boro straight away? An opportunity like this wouldn't come along every day. The club thought they needed him, and there seemed to be very little to lose.

"OK. I'm in," he said. "I'll do it."

The first thing he needed to do was announce his official retirement from his playing career. Then he could go about establishing a playing style, looking into transfers and making some big decisions.

Middlesbrough had lost a number of players over the summer, including Jimmy Floyd Hasselbaink and Doriva – as well as Gareth himself.

Gareth started by recruiting centre-backs Jonathan Woodgate and Robert Huth. He worked on setting up a disciplined team, with a hard-working defence and midfield. He wanted them to keep games tight, defending well, and then using the skills of Downing and Mendieta to create chances for strikers like Yakubu and Mark Viduka.

The first game, a 3-2 defeat at Reading, was a disappointment. The next game, his first at home, was an even tougher match. They were taking on last year's champions, Chelsea.

Once more, Middlesbrough got off to the worst possible start, with an early Andriy Shevchenko goal giving Chelsea the lead.

Gareth sat on the sidelines for most of the first half, only occasionally shouting instructions to his team. He glanced nervously over at José Mourinho every time the Chelsea manager rose from his seat. Mourinho had already won multiple Premier League titles and a Champions League, even though he wasn't that much older than Gareth himself.

At half-time, 'Boro trailed, but it was only by one goal.

"Look guys," Gareth told his players. "If we get a goal, there's no reason why we can't go on to get a win from this. We're created chances – we just need to convert them."

As the second half began, coach Steve Round spoke up. "We need to make changes soon, Gareth," he insisted. "Get Viduka on, maybe Morrison."

"Give it some time," Gareth murmured.

After twenty minutes or so, Gareth finally blinked. Mark Viduka and Lee Cattermole were summoned from the bench and he switched from the five-at-the-back formation he had been using and turned to two up front. Yakubu and Viduka were similar strikers in style, and Gareth knew they were going to be physically a handful for the Chelsea defence.

"If we can get crosses in, we'll get a goal."

With 10 minutes left, 'Boro won a free kick on the far side of the box. The delivery was perfect and Emanuel Pogatetz rose high in the air, powering a huge header into the back of the net.

The Riverside Stadium erupted into a wall of noise. The scores might be level, but now the momentum was with 'Boro. They were all over Chelsea, piling forward in huge numbers.

"Keep going, boys!" Gareth roared from the bench. It occurred to him that perhaps he should settle for a draw, but he dismissed the thought. He wanted the win.

As the match crept into added time, 'Boro once more fired a ball into the box. Yakubu controlled it on his thigh and flicked it into Viduka, who spun and fired the ball into the back of the net.

2-1! 'Boro had come from behind to clinch a famous win over the champions.

Gareth rose from his seat, punching the air, and turning to the fans, gesturing to them, firing them up. He had announced himself as 'Boro manager with a huge win.

But what really surprised him was how the win made him feel. He'd thought that managing a team, rather than playing on the pitch, might not bring him the same rewards. Now he realised that it actually felt better. They were all working together, as a team, and he was the guy calling the shots. When it went well, it felt like nothing else.

So this is what management is like, he thought. He couldn't wait to see where it would take him.

10
THAT'S FOOTBALL

February 2007, Stamford Bridge, Chelsea, England
Chelsea v Middlesbrough

The win against Chelsea hadn't quite set the tone for the rest of Middlesbrough's season. Just five days later, they were thrashed 4-0 at home by Portsmouth.

It was followed by a four-match winless run. Gareth continually tinkered with the team, going for two up top, then a three at the back, a 4-3-3, rotating his midfielders, his back four …

Eventually, they ended the poor run with a win against Everton. The rest of the season continued in a similar way. A win or two was followed by a run of defeats or draws. No matter what Gareth did, he couldn't work out how to get results consistently.

Eventually, he turned to his former boss, the current England manager, Steve McClaren, for help.

"So how do we turn it around, Steve?" Gareth asked. "I've tried everything – so many different formations. We get a good run, and then it seems to go completely wrong."

"Are you using the same formation against every team?" McClaren asked. "Sometimes you need to change things, alter your tactics depending on who you're playing."

"So … drop players who've had a good game, just so we can have a formation that fits the opposition? That doesn't seem right."

"Those are the tough calls a manager has to make," McClaren replied. "It's not about being fair. Having your 'best' team on the pitch is no good if they don't win the game. Set your team up to exploit the weaknesses in the opposition. And if they've got some dangerous players, work out how to neutralise them." McClaren looked at Gareth and grinned. "Mind you, doing that doesn't always get you friends."

Gareth wasn't convinced, but he tried to follow the advice. Against Sheffield United, who had slow full-backs, he put in some of his quicker players, telling them to get the ball out wide. For the next game against Charlton, he put in more midfielders, so they could control the game from the centre. 'Boro won both games 3-1, even though Gareth had to drop players who'd expected to get a start. He could see them looking at him from the bench, questioning his choices.

It was a difficult situation and not one that he felt comfortable with, but it was working. Middlesbrough had moved into the top half of the table. The run continued with a 5-1 win over Bolton, followed by draws with Portsmouth and Arsenal.

The next game was away to Chelsea, the team that Gareth had beaten to announce himself as 'Boro manager. Chelsea were right at the top of the table and in the thick of a title race. Without the Riverside crowd, this would be tough.

"So, what are we thinking?" Gareth asked, conferring with his team of coaches, including his new assistant, Colin Cooper.

"In August, we looked very dangerous when we went to two up front," Colin replied. "Viduka, Yakubu. They found it hard to match our physicality."

"We don't want to get drawn into a midfield battle," Gareth mused. That was where Chelsea had far superior players, including Makélélé, Lampard and Essien. But if they got it out wide and got crosses in, it might give them the advantage. It didn't matter how good you were – if a cross was put in the box, it was just a striker against a defender.

That was the key message Gareth relayed to his players. "At the end of the day, lads," he told them, "there's just 22 players out there. Anything can happen. Ignore the crowd, ignore everything else once you step out on that pitch. Just focus on the game."

"We've beaten them once before," Emanuel Pogatetz added. "And we deserved that win. We can do it again."

For 40 minutes, the teams were level – in fact, 'Boro were on top. Viduka headed just wide from six yards, and Yakubu had a chance that was palmed away by Čech.

Then, just seconds before half-time, Didier Drogba opened the scoring with a moment of brilliance. From a free-kick, he whipped the ball under the wall and into the far corner.

Gareth turned away in disgust, shaking his head.

"There's nothing you can do about that," one of the coaches said to him. "Just brilliant."

" 'Could have taken our chances," Gareth muttered.

In the second half, Chelsea sealed it with an own goal from Abel Xavier, followed by a late Drogba free-kick.

Middlesbrough had lost momentum after the first goal. Gareth had seen it in his players' eyes at half-time. Before the game, they had believed they could win it, but after that goal they had given up.

Gareth sat in the dressing room after the game, remembering the other bit of advice McClaren had given him. "Sometimes, you'll come up against a better team," he'd said. "Everything will go their way, and nothing will go yours. No matter what you do. That's just football."

11
BUILDING THE SQUAD

May 2008, Riverside Stadium, Middlesbrough, England
Middlesbrough v Man City

In the end, 'Boro finished safely mid-table. The close gave Gareth the chance to dip back into the transfer market. A year ago, he'd not been sure exactly what he was looking for, but now he was certain.

The first issue was the lack of strikers. Mark Viduka had moved to rivals Newcastle, and Malcolm Christie and Danny Graham had also both left the club. Then Yakubu was picked up for one of the highest fees 'Boro had received for a player, joining Everton for £11.25 million.

The departures made it easier. Gareth no longer had to work out who to sell – he just needed to think about who he wanted to sign.

The first new arrival was Jérémie Aliadière, the French U21 striker who had won the Premier League with Arsenal. He was joined by the more experienced additions, Tuncay, Mido and Gary O'Neil.

Nevertheless, the process left Gareth frustrated. "How are we supposed to build something, to improve," he asked his assistant, Malcolm Crosby, "if we can't build our squad the way we want? We're just replacing every player who goes out. We're static."

"That's the way it is at our level," Malcolm replied. "We don't get to choose. We just have to do our best."

"How did McClaren do it?" Gareth mused. "He got us into Europe. We won the cup."

"Bit of luck – sometimes you get the signings right, the tactics right … " Malcolm shrugged.

"But there has to be a plan?" Gareth asked. "You can't just go in randomly and pray for a bit of luck."

He was trying to build a squad that had the necessary depth to lift 'Boro above their mid-table finish of last year. Gradually, he realised that, to do this, he'd have to work it out for himself.

He began by looking at each of his players, identifying strengths and weaknesses. There was creative talent in the likes of Stewart Downing and Julio Arca, and defensively they were sound, with David Wheater, Pogatetz, Luke Young and Jonathan Woodgate. The problems were going to be getting goals. It was going to be a case of just getting as many new names into the squad as possible.

At the halfway point in January, 'Boro were 14th. They had struggled at the start of the campaign, but then they'd recovered, with wins over Arsenal, Derby and Portsmouth.

In the January transfer window, the board showed their faith in him, letting him spend £12 million on Brazilian striker Afonso Alves – a man who'd scored over 40 goals in the Eredivisie.

But despite four new strikers in all, 'Boro were still struggling. Wins were followed by defeats, and defeats by draws. They were static, going nowhere in the table.

So in the final game of the season, at home to Man City, there was almost nothing to play for. But, Gareth knew that they had to give the fans something more, something to inspire them for next season.

"Let's give a good send off, guys," he told the players before the game. "The fans have supported us all year and they deserve a good win."

The game got off to an almost perfect start when, in the first 15 minutes, Richard Dunne took out Tuncay in the penalty area. Stewart Downing converted the resulting penalty and Dunne was given a red card. There was an opportunity now for 'Boro to run riot, to rack up a big score.

Alves scored a second before half-time, and then the goals came piling in. Three, four, five, six, seven … Gareth couldn't believe it. He hadn't been part of a huge win like this since he'd played in the under-12s.

The final score was 8-1 – with a hat-trick for Alves, a double for Stewart Downing and a goal for new signing Jérémie Aliadière.

It was 'Boro's biggest win in a long time, and their biggest ever in the Premier League. They hadn't just beaten City – they had humiliated them. This, surely, set the tone for next year.

There was a smile on his face as Gareth watched his players celebrating the win. Perhaps, next year, he could do more than just stay in the middle of the table. Perhaps he could turn 'Boro into a serious top-level team.

12
DOWN – AND OUT

October 2009, Riverside Stadium, Middlesbrough, England
Middlesbrough v Derby

"Gareth, Steve wants to see you. In his private box."

Those were the words that Gareth had been dreading for over a year now. He knew exactly what they meant. There was no good reason why Middlesbrough chairman Steve Gibson would want to see him in his private box after a routine 2-0 win over Derby.

Gareth had been confident with his business in the

summer. He was going to revitalise the 'Boro squad. Out went defensive midfielders Lee Cattermole and George Boateng. In came excitement, in Marvin Emnes, and risk-taking, in younger players like Didier Digard and Justin Hoyte.

But after a decent start, results quickly turned. Between November and February, 'Boro failed to win a single game, scoring just five goals in that time.

Gareth had no idea how to rectify the situation. The 8-1 victory over Man City seemed so distant now. It wasn't just the big teams that they were losing to. They were being battered too by teams at their own level, with heavy 3-0 defeats to West Brom and Fulham.

After nine seasons in the Premier League, Middlesbrough were relegated on the final day of the 2008/9 season.

As captain, Gareth had lifted the club's first major trophy in over 100 years. Now, as manager, he had got the club relegated.

"Why don't you step down?" a lot of his friends had asked him. "There's no shame in walking away – especially when it's clearly not working out."

"As long as I'm contracted to work here, I will," he'd insisted. "I think I'm the best man for the job, the man who can get us back into the Premier League."

Anyway, Gareth wasn't going to walk away from a problem that he believed he'd created. That wasn't in his nature.

There was a lot of change at the club over the summer. Understandably, very few players were willing to remain at the club, given their relegation, and Stewart Downing, Robert Huth and Afonso Alves had all left.

Even though it was a very different squad from the one Gareth had managed in previous years, they remained near the top of the Championship and, after today's 2-0 win over Derby, they'd moved into fourth spot.

So Gareth was surprised to find himself climbing the steps towards Steve Gibson's private box. He'd expected this call earlier in the year, when 'Boro had gone so many games without winning. He'd also expected it after their relegation, or even during the summer. But, not now.

"Gareth," Steve said, not making eye contact as Gareth entered his room. "Take a seat."

Gareth slumped into a chair. If he hadn't already known where this meeting was going, he knew now.

"Steve," he sighed. "I know it's not been easy, but I really think I'm the one who can get us back … "

He trailed off, looking at Steve's face. Obviously the decision had already been made.

"Football-wise," Steve told him, "this was an easy decision. But, personally, this is the toughest call I've made in all my years in the business. I'm sorry Gareth, but we're letting you go. We're going another way."

Gareth stood up. He didn't need to hear any more – he didn't want to drag this out. He just wanted to get out of there.

"Thank you for everything, Steve," he said, shaking the chairman's hand. "It's been a pleasure."

Then he just turned and walked away. As he stumbled down the steps, the events of the last year played out in his mind. What could he have done differently? He had no idea.

Nor did he have any idea what he was going to do next.

13
NOT EASY

September 2013, Madejski Stadium, Reading, England
England U21 v Moldova U21

For four years, Gareth had been a bystander in the world of football. As the man who'd relegated Middlesbrough and then had been sacked, leaving them struggling in the Championship, he had no interest in rejoining the football world, either as a manager or in any other role.

His first six months outside football had turned into a year – and the year had turned into two. He'd started working as an occasional pundit for ITV, watching the England games and passing on his expertise and experience as a player. He'd started working with the FA too, helping develop players, and then joining the team of advisors helping Roy Hodgson plan out the future England team.

That was the role that finally got him back into management. For the past several years, the England U21 team had been managed by Stuart Pearce. He had taken them to a European Championship final, where they had been soundly beaten by Germany.

That had been the high point of Pearce's reign, and in the summer of 2013, after another poor U21 showing at a European Championship, he was sacked.

This left a vacancy in a key role in the England set-up. The U21 manager was crucial in readying players to move from the youth teams into the first team. It was a role that Gareth felt was perfect for him.

He decided that he wanted to do it.

There were several sets of interviews with a number of the movers and shakers at the FA, including Trevor Brooking and Dan Ashworth.

There were several other candidates for the job – René Meulensteen, Steve McClaren and Peter Taylor amongst them. All of them had more managerial experience than Gareth, and he knew there was nothing he could do about that. But none of them had his passion. Gareth had been an England player – and, perhaps crucially, he'd been involved in that Euro 96 penalty shoot-out. He knew what it was like to let his team down, to lose with England. He knew how much it mattered.

A few weeks went by before Gareth was contacted. The job was his.

But now he'd been offered it, was he really sure he wanted it? Should he accept the offer? There was only one man he needed to speak to now – an old friend and team-mate, a man who knew a lot about the U21s. His predecessor, Stuart Pearce.

"Stuart," he said, as his friend picked up the phone. "How are you? Can we have a chat?"

"The Under-21s?" Stuart guessed. Rumours had been rumbling around in the last couple of weeks and Gareth had been the favourite for a while now.

"Yeah," Gareth replied, sheepishly. "I hope there's no hard feelings, me taking your old job and everything."

"None at all," Stuart laughed. "That's not why you've phoned, though, is it?"

"Not exactly." Gareth paused. "It's a tough job, isn't it? I watched you do it for a long time. It looked like a lot of hard work and effort, without much reward. Have I got that right?"

"Pretty much," Stuart said. "But there's some good moments. We got a final. And I was able to work with some of the best youngsters in the country. Some of them went on to win Premier Leagues, Champions Leagues. You get to be a part of all that."

"Maybe one day a World Cup," Gareth mused.

"That's the aim," Stuart said. "You work with Roy. You're trying to build a team that wins the World Cup in 10 years' time, instead of now. That's not easy."

Gareth knew it would be a tough job, especially if somebody like Stuart Pearce had been worn down by it. But he was itching to get back into football, into management, once again. So he signed on the dotted line. He was the new manager of the England U21s.

His first game was at home against Moldova U21. Managing a national side was quite different to being the manager of a club side. You couldn't bring in signings to fill positions you were weak in, or to complement other players. You could only work with what was available to you.

You also couldn't watch the players day in, day out, in training. You could only see them in matches – and sometimes they weren't even playing. So you had to rely on advice from scouts or coaches.

And all that was before your best players got poached by the senior side – or, worse still, by another country.

The first thing Gareth did was to write out what he believed to be his best starting line-up, thinking that he would be working with this team for the next two or three years. He quickly realised that he would almost never have all those players available to him at the same time. He would have to adapt.

Eventually, he was able to settle on a core line-up. He had the quality of Saido Berahino, Zaha and Nathan Redmond in the forward line. There was quality in midfield, with James Ward-Prowse and Tom Carroll.

And then, at the back, Luke Shaw, Michael Keane and John Stones were as good as they got at that age.

He couldn't wait to put on a show and blow the Moldovans away. When Saido Berahino put England ahead inside 15 minutes, it seemed as if the floodgates were going to open. But then, nothing. England had a lot of possession and they created chances, but they didn't score again for the rest of the game. Gareth's big opening had finished in a limp 1-0 win.

He couldn't work out what had gone so wrong. On paper, it was a quality team. But on the pitch, the players didn't seem to gel. There wasn't any chemistry, any link-ups, between the players.

At club level you could work on this in training for a few weeks, letting the players get to know each other, learning each other's playing styles. But England now had just three days until their next game, after which they'd be sent back to their various clubs, where they all played very different styles of football for very different teams.

Gareth slumped into a seat in the dressing room and sighed.

International management was going to be hard.

14
RESULT

May 2016, Parc des Sports, Avignon, France
Toulon Tournament Final, England U21 v France U21

Slowly, Gareth was starting to get to grips with his team. Some players he lost almost instantly, before they'd really become a part of his team. Harry Kane, Raheem Sterling and John Stones were all quickly moved into the first team squad. He barely saw Marcus Rashford or Dele Alli before they were scooped up too.

Others departed for different reasons. Some became

too old to be part of his team and he had to let them go. Some were a bit too volatile – difficult personalities who he had to let go for the greater good of the squad.

Nevertheless, he was building a solid core. Nathaniel Chalobah and James Ward-Prowse were ever-present in the heart of midfield. Nathan Redmond and Ruben Loftus-Cheek added flair and dynamism further forward. At the back, Calum Chambers had vast experience for his age, bringing that into every game.

But there were still disappointments.

In the Euro 2015 competition, Gareth had breezed through the qualifiers, just as his predecessor, Stuart Pearce, had done and, just like his predecessor, they had then struggled in the final tournament. They had lost narrowly to Portugal in the opening game, before bouncing back and winning their second game against Sweden with a late goal.

Then, in the final game, they'd been soundly beaten by a fast, dynamic, Italy team. It had been a comfortable 3-1 win and England's goal had come late on. They had never really been in the game.

After the tournament, criticism rained in from all

sides. Some said that Gareth had picked the wrong squad, that he wasn't the right man for the job. Others asked why Jack Wilshere and Raheem Sterling hadn't been included. Gareth was in danger of going the same way as his friend and predecessor, Stuart Pearce.

He had to rebuild.

"We had a decent run in the qualifiers," Gareth told his assistant, Steve Holland. "There's no point chucking out all the players that got us there."

"We've got to think realistically," Holland replied. "We know Kane and Stones are going up. Lingard, Ings and Jenkinson will all be too old soon. That's a lot of players we're losing."

"We still have a good core," Gareth insisted. "Enough to have done better than we did."

"I thought it wasn't about results?"

"No, it's not," Gareth mused. "But we're preparing the players for winning a tournament with the England first team. They need to be ready for tournament football. We want them to experience winning a tournament, going all the way, lifting the trophy."

"Toulon is next summer," Holland replied. "Let's

focus on that. It's got even more of a World Cup feel, with teams from all over."

"There, results *will* matter," Gareth said.

The Toulon Tournament was one of the most prestigious youth tournaments in world football. Independent of both UEFA and FIFA, it included teams from all around the world. It was an opportunity to test yourself against teams that weren't part of the usual European circuit – teams from South America, Asia and Africa, for example.

England were drawn into a five-team group alongside Portugal, Japan, Guinea and Paraguay. A year ago, they had lost to Portugal in the opening game of a tournament. This time, they beat them 1-0. They followed it up with a 7-1 win over Guinea, a 4-0 win over Paraguay and a 1-0 win over Japan, getting them to the final, where they would be taking on the hosts, France.

The final was played on a small pitch on a cloudy, overcast day. Nothing about it suggested that this was the final of a major international tournament, or how important it was to Gareth's future in the England setup.

He'd gone with his strongest team. Jordan Pickford

in goal, Chambers and Kortney Hause in defence. Loftus-Cheek, Lewis Baker, Ward-Prowse and Nathan Redmond were his creative quartet. He knew that the French team were strong, but he had faith that his team could break the curse of English teams at tournaments like this one and bring home the trophy.

England got off to a perfect start inside 10 minutes. Ward-Prowse's floated ball was directed towards the onrushing Lewis Baker, who met it with his head and looped it over the French keeper. 1-0.

"Come on!" Gareth shouted, pumping his fist and high-fiving Steve Holland.

"Long way to go yet, Gaz," Holland warned.

France came back strongly, but then, a few minutes before half-time, England broke again. The ball bounced through for Ruben Loftus-Cheek in the box and he chipped it over the keeper. England had doubled their advantage and there was now just 45 minutes of football between them and the trophy.

The second half was tight. With a couple of minutes left to play, France pulled a goal back. Now England had to hold on.

"Time for the change," Gareth said, turning to Steve Holland. "We're not losing this."

He called his centre-back, Jack Stephens, off the bench, putting him on as another defensive change. He was a tall, powerful defender, who could meet every aerial challenge. It wasn't pretty, but Gareth wasn't losing this game.

The three minutes that remained seemed to take an eternity to tick over. Gareth stood on the edge of his technical area, arms by his side, fists clenched, desperate not to show his nervousness to the players – but also desperate for the ref to blow the whistle.

At last, the whistle went and Gareth sunk to his knees, before being swept up in the celebrations. The England U21s had won a tournament. It might not have been the Euros, but it was a major tournament nonetheless.

Tonight, his players would have medals around their necks and their hands on a trophy.

Next, they would have to do it with the senior side.

15
WHATEVER YOU DO, DO IT SOON

October 2016, Wembley Stadium, London, England
World Cup Qualifier, England v Malta

A month after Gareth's U21s had lifted their first trophy, beating Portugal and France to win the Toulon Tournament, the senior side went to France for their own major tournament, the 2016 European Championships.

Gareth wasn't part of England manager Roy Hodgson's coaching team, so he watched most of the finals at home on TV. He celebrated England's dramatic win over Wales in the group stage, but was dismayed by what he saw in draws with Russia and Slovakia. England eventually made a last-16 exit, humiliated by a 2-1 loss to minnows Iceland.

Gareth slumped in his chair as he watched the game at home. It was bad enough to lose like this, but he knew what it would mean for Roy. He was unlikely to be England manager for much longer.

"Are you going to apply for it?" Gareth's assistant, Steve Holland, asked him when they next met up.

Roy had announced his decision to resign as England manager just minutes after the Iceland game. He'd had three major tournaments in charge of the senior team, and he'd failed to get any further than the quarter-finals in any of them.

"The England job?" Gareth asked, pretending he didn't know what his assistant was talking about.

"Yes, the England job," Steve Holland laughed. "They're talking about Steve Bruce, Sam Allardyce. You've got to be in there too, surely. You know the system inside-out."

"I don't know." Gareth admitted. "I'll probably try, but they'll probably want more experience. Last year, we did just as badly at the Euros. That's not a great recommendation."

"But we won Toulon," Holland said. "And you've got a great relationship already with a lot of the players."

"Let's wait and see."

As Gareth had guessed, the FA wanted to go with experience. The job was given to Sam Allardyce, a man with a wealth of experience, having managed West Ham, Crystal Palace and Bolton.

His reign lasted one game and less than 10 weeks. After a scandal involving undercover journalists and allegations of selling information, he was sacked.

As Gareth saw it, England had gone from stability under Hodgson to chaos and no manager in the space of just a month.

He was the first person on the phone to FA director Dan Ashworth.

"I guess you want the job now, Gareth?" Ashworth sighed. "We haven't started the interviews again … "

"No," Gareth said firmly. "I don't care who you get in. Just, whatever you do, do it soon. You've got World Cup-winning youngsters in that squad, players of incredible quality. Do not waste them. Promise me you won't waste them, Dan."

"We'll try," Ashworth replied, sheepishly.

A few days later, Ashworth called Gareth back. "Gareth," he said. "Look, I'll be honest. Initially you weren't part of our plans. We thought you were too young and, frankly, your managerial experience isn't amazing.

"But ... " Ashworth paused. "We've had a change of heart. The way you spoke the other day was more passionate than any of the candidates we've had in here. Look, it'll only be on a temporary basis. You'll have four games in charge. Impress us in those, and we can probably offer you the permanent job."

Gareth took a deep breath. From nowhere, he was being offered the England job, even if it was only temporary.

"And if I don't do well?" he asked Ashworth.

"Let's not worry about that," Ashworth replied.

Gareth wasn't going to make any major changes to the team itself – that was pretty well established. On the coaching side, he chose Steve Holland as his right-hand man.

"We need to discuss our first squad," Gareth told him. "It's the one that sets the tone, the one that people remember."

"Well, some are obvious, surely," Holland replied. "Kane, Walker, Rooney, Sterling. They're all nailed on."

"I'm sticking with Rooney as captain," Gareth added. "This isn't the time for huge changes like that."

"Hart in goal," Holland mused. "Henderson and Eric Dier in the middle."

"Here's my two riskier choices," Gareth said. "Rashford and Lingard. Let's bring them back in."

Gareth's squad announcement was met with a tirade of abuse. He'd experienced criticism in the past, but it was nothing like this. Every decision he had made was met with a furious response. Some said he'd picked too many United players. Others said he hadn't picked enough. And on and on. It was clear that, whatever he did, he would be facing a wall of criticism.

It was a wake-up call. Every decision he made from now on, every tactic, every team selection, was going to be scrutinised, put under the microscope.

The first game was at home against Malta. It was a

game England were expected to win comfortably, and Gareth knew that. They had no Harry Kane due to injury, but they still had a strong front three, with Sturridge, Lingard and Theo Walcott.

"Look, lads," Gareth told them before the game. "I know you've seen a lot of change with managers. I don't know how long it's going to be for, but for now, I'm the manager. So let's get to it."

"The boss is right." Rooney added. "Let's get fully behind him."

"Today isn't just about the result," Gareth continued. "It's about entertaining the fans, impressing them. Let's get the ball forward, create chances. I want goals."

England won the game by two goals, both scored in the first half with Daniel Sturridge and Dele Alli converting two of the numerous chances England created. It wasn't a huge win and it wasn't the free-flowing, attacking display that Gareth had wanted.

But it was a win.

Gareth had his first win as England manager. He just prayed it was the first of many.

16
SHOOT-OUT

July 2018, Spartak Stadium, Moscow, Russia
Round of 16, World Cup 2018, England v Colombia

"What do we know about Colombia?" Gareth asked, glancing over at the notepad where his assistant, Steve Holland, was furiously scribbling down notes.

"Bad-tempered," Holland shrugged. "Rodríguez, Bacca, Falcao. Good players. Hard to beat."

"Well, Rodríguez is injured, so we can ignore him. And Bacca is benched."

Gareth wasn't sure what else Holland had scribbled down on that pad. After all, the game was only five minutes old. The truth was, Gareth knew everything there was to know about Colombia. As soon as the World Cup last-16 ties had been confirmed, he'd found out everything he could about the South American side.

Even so, he kept asking Holland what he knew about their opponents. He was hoping that something would leap out at him, some little detail that he'd missed – the secret to beating Colombia.

"Do you remember our first game?" Gareth asked Holland, not looking over at him but keeping his eyes fixed on the game in front of him.

"Malta," Holland replied. "Yeah, of course. Why?"

"I never thought I'd get the job permanently." Gareth shrugged. "And that team was so different. Rooney, Sturridge, Hart, Walcott. It was unrecognisable."

"Four at the back," Holland chuckled.

"Exactly," Gareth said, shaking his head.

It was only in the last few months that his England side had reverted to a three-at-the-back formation, using wing-backs and pushing Kyle Walker back as a right-sided centre-back. So far it had worked wonders.

There were other changes too. Harry Kane was the new England captain and he'd been in sparkling form, with five goals at this tournament so far.

Not long into the first half, Gareth turned to Holland. "Let's push it out wide more," he said. "We're going too central, playing into their hands."

It didn't take long for his instructions to get out on the pitch. Kieran Trippier got out on the overlap and his whipped cross was headed just over the bar by Kane.

"We need to take those, we need to take those," Gareth muttered, holding his head in his hands. He was right to be worried. Chances were few and far between, and the game was broken up by a number of fouls.

"We're doing fine, lads," he told his players at half-time. "Just don't lose your heads. They're going to try and wind you up, get in your face, push you into a red card. Don't rise to it. We keep ourselves focused."

Ten minutes into the second half, Kane was dragged to the floor by Carlos Sánchez, and the referee pointed to the penalty spot. The Colombians were furious. They protested for several minutes, surrounding the referee.

"They're kicking up the penalty spot," Steve Holland said, gesturing to the Colombians in the box.

"Tell the players to calm down," Gareth said. "Get Dele and Lingard out of there."

Despite the attempts by Colombia to ruin the penalty spot, Kane was unstoppable. He comfortably added his sixth goal of the tournament. England had the lead.

"He is so important," Gareth murmured to himself.

Should England now push for two, or just try to hold on? Gareth decided to leave things unchanged. With 30 minutes left, one goal wasn't enough. They needed another.

As Colombia pushed, Gareth started to make changes. Dier on for Alli, Jamie Vardy on for Sterling.

With the game in added time, Pickford was forced into a fantastic save, giving Colombia a corner. Gareth watched the yellow shirts streaming forward for the kick, feeling a sick knot in the pit of his stomach. England were so close …

The cross was brilliant. Gareth watched as the huge presence of Yerry Mina rose in the air and connected with it with his head. The ball cannoned off him, bounced high into the air and over the England man on the line. Colombia had equalised.

As the Colombians celebrated, Gareth watched his own players' heads drop. There was going to be 30 minutes of extra time now. He had to pick his players up again.

He gathered them together, feeling their pain and their disappointment. "We've beaten them once," he told them. "We're so close. We're the better team. We're the fitter team – they've been doing all the running. Now let's go out and beat them again."

Now things had turned around. England were now the team pushing for a goal – and Colombia were the team defending hard. Gareth threw on Danny Rose for Ashley Young, and then with five minutes remaining, with penalties in mind, Rashford was on, replacing defender Kyle Walker.

They really didn't want to end up in a penalty shootout. England hadn't won one since 1996, and Gareth himself knew the heartache of a defeat.

With both sets of players exhausted, after extra time the scores were still level. It would go to a shootout.

"I know we have a list, guys," Gareth told his players. "But does anyone feel up to taking one? And anyone feel they can't?"

Jamie Vardy put his hand up. "I can't, boss," he said, pointing at his leg. "I'm finished."

"OK, that's fine," Gareth nodded. "Anyone else?" Nobody said anything.

"We know the order," he said. "Pick your spot, hit it hard. We've practised this, we know what we need to do."

Colombia were up first. Falcao converted. Next it was Kane, England's regular penalty taker.

"He'll score," Gareth said confidently. He did.

Cuadrado, Rashford and Luis Muriel all scored next. Colombia were leading 3-2. Jordan Henderson walked up to the spot. He didn't strike it cleanly and the Colombian keeper met it with a big hand, tipping it round the post. Henderson had missed.

Mateus Uribe was up next. England needed a big save from Pickford. The shot was strong and powerful – well out of the reach of Pickford – but it was too high and slammed into the crossbar, before bouncing back out. Both teams had now missed one each. Game on.

Next up was Kieran Trippier, who planted a high, powerful shot into the top corner. 3-3.

Now Carlos Bacca was up for Colombia. His penalty was right down the middle, but Pickford got a hand to it and palmed it away. Colombia had missed.

If Eric Dier scored, England would win.

Gareth almost wanted to run out there and take it himself. He couldn't bear seeing this kind of pressure on his players. After all, he'd been there himself.

Dier took a few steps back, the eyes of the nation on him. He charged forward and hit it hard, towards the bottom corner. It was perfect.

As the net rippled, Gareth sank to his knees, his coaching staff charging forward around him. It felt like redemption for his own miss in 1996. He had guided England to a penalty shootout win.

As he celebrated, he heard his song ringing around the stadium. "Southgate, you're the one! Football's coming home again!"

Today, he and his team had created a great moment in England's football history. He just hoped it wasn't his last.

17
NAÏVE

July 2018, Luzhniki Stadium, Moscow, Russia
World Cup Semi-Final, England v Croatia

Gareth sat in the dressing room and looked at the Croatia teamsheet. "Now *that's* a midfield," he remarked to Steve Holland. "Modrić, Rakitić, Brozović."

"Kovačić on the bench." Holland replied. He glanced round the room, making sure that nobody could overhear them, then whispered, "Any of them would walk into our team."

"We've got other strengths," Gareth replied, before standing up to address the players.

"We're 10 minutes from the biggest game in our history," Gareth told them. "The biggest game for England since 1990. We've got an opportunity to reach our first final since '66." He paused for a moment. Was it dramatic effect, or was he too thinking about the implications of that statement?

"But put history aside," he said. "This is just a game, just a match against a very good team. A very beatable team. They've gone to extra time and pens in every one of their matches so far. They will be tired. We have to take advantage of that."

"He's right," Steve Holland added. "As the time ticks on, we'll need to be ready to step up. Exhaust them."

"Their midfield is strong," Gareth conceded. "They'll want to play it between the three of them. Modrić will want to dictate. We don't let him. We get it to our wide players, get Harry and Raheem in the game."

England started with intensity. Lingard and Alli exchanged passes on the edge of the box, before the latter was tripped by Modrić. The free kick was taken by

Kieran Trippier, who whipped it perfectly into the top corner. England had the lead.

"Boys, we want a second!" Gareth shouted over to his team. He didn't want a repeat of Colombia – he wasn't sure he could take a second penalty shootout.

A few minutes before half-time, England almost got their second. The ball was scooped into Kane in the penalty area, but his first shot was saved and his second whistled up off the keeper and onto the bar.

"Why didn't he square it!" Gareth fumed. "Sterling was right there!" Gareth knew that that miss was going to be crucial. This was definitely a game of fine margins.

At half-time, Gareth urged his players on. He wanted them to keep pressing, keep the energy up, but they had already started to sit back. They had started defending their 1-0 lead, rather than pushing for a second.

He only made a single sub, swapping Rashford for Sterling. These were the players that had earned their place in the team and, looking at his bench, he didn't see any options to change things. Squad depth was a problem for England.

In the second half, Croatia came back strongly and,

with 20 minutes to go, they struck. A cross from Vrsaljko beat the England defence and was guided home by Ivan Perišić. Now Croatia were level.

A moment later, Perišić hit the post. Croatia were pushing for a second.

England managed to hold on, and once more the game went into extra time. Now was the time for changes. Gareth threw on Danny Rose and Eric Dier, making like-for-like changes. There was no need to change the system.

England were better in extra time, but it wasn't enough. One England switch-off at the back allowed Mandžukić in. He struck a low shot into the far corner, putting Croatia into the lead.

As he watched the Croatian celebrations, Gareth knew that the game was done. Modrić had controlled the game since almost the very beginning. England had been naïve – Croatia had been street smart.

"More strength in depth," he sighed. "More control."

"We should be proud," Steve Holland insisted. "We've done so well."

"We can do better," Gareth said. "We *will* do better."

18
A GREAT TEAM

October 2018, Benito Villamarín Stadium, Seville, Spain
UEFA Nations League, England v Spain

Gareth looked around the room at his players. Three months ago, they had reached the semi-finals of the World Cup, where they had been solidly beaten by Croatia. Since then, there had been a lot of changes.

Joe Gomez, Ben Chilwell, Harry Winks and Jadon Sancho had all been integrated into the squad, whilst Ashley Young, Jamie Vardy and Gary Cahill had been moved on. There were talented youngsters lurking in the England youth teams – Gareth was keen to make the most of them.

Since the Croatia game, he'd become aware of an issue that had plagued England during that semi-final – naïvety. After the opening goal of that match, Croatia had controlled the game. England had had to chase it, leaving gaps at the back. They'd panicked. Croatia had controlled the ball and exposed the gaps.

Gareth's squad now had a lot of attacking players, and he wanted to take advantage of that. For the World Cup, he had put defensive solidarity over attacking prowess. Now it was time to reverse that. So he switched to a 4-3-3 formation, planning to utilise Rashford, Sterling and Kane as a dynamic and pacy front three. It added more midfielders, which he hoped would help England control the game from the middle.

"A few months ago, we reached a World Cup semi-final," he began, looking around at his players. "We were beaten. In the third-place playoff, we lost again. If we're going to be a truly great team, we need to beat the other big teams," he added. "So far, we've lost every time. I consider us a great team. Let's prove that tonight."

He paused, making sure everybody was paying attention.

"Spain have dominated world football for four years. They still have Ramos, Busquets, Thiago, de Gea. They are without doubt a quality team. If we want to consider ourselves their equal, we have to win tonight."

As the team headed towards the tunnel, Gareth called Eric Dier aside.

"Control them in that midfield tonight," he told him. "Be combative, aggressive – don't let them get comfortable on the ball. That's their strength."

He knew Spain were the pass masters of European football. They were able to control games as well as any other team in Europe. If England could go toe-to-toe with them, then they could prove to the world that they could compete with the big teams – even the passing teams.

England made the perfect start. It started from the back, with the ball fed into Harry Kane. His pass was brilliant and released Rashford, who zipped it inside for Raheem Sterling. His first touch was great, his second was a powerful shot that flew into the top corner. It was his first goal for England in a long, long time.

It was a goal that Spain themselves would be proud of, but Gareth Southgate's England had scored it. And all within the first 15 minutes.

Another 15 minutes later, England doubled their lead. Once more, it came from Jordan Pickford, whose long ball was brought down by Kane. He was direct and brilliant – his pass fed the onrushing Rashford, who tucked it into the far corner.

But there was still more to come. Kane set up Sterling, who tapped in to make it 3-0.

England weren't just beating Spain – they were humiliating them in their own country. They were showing that they could take on the great teams and beat them.

"That's another one for the critics, Gareth," Steve Holland said, at the end of the game. "That's not just luck."

"We've got a squad to really win something," Gareth replied. "We have to make the most of it."

19
SEMI-FINALIST

July 2021, Wembley Stadium, London, England
Euro 2020 Semi-Final, England v Denmark

"It's good to have fans back properly," Gareth remarked.

Wembley was as loud as he'd ever heard it. It was even louder than it had been last week, when his England side had outplayed, outfought and outclassed Germany to win 2-0. Since then, they had gone to Rome and thrashed Ukraine 4-0. Now they were back on home turf, in front of over 60,000 fans, most of them English.

England had come a long way since 2018. The "three-at-the-back" had been replaced by a vibrant 4-2-3-1. Kane, Sterling, Walker, Maguire, Stones and Pickford were all still present, and they formed the backbone, the leadership group, of this England side.

For this game, the youngsters Bukayo Saka, Declan Rice and Mason Mount were starting. Phil Foden, Jack Grealish and Jadon Sancho were on the bench.

Gareth now had options. He remembered that World Cup semi in 2018, when he'd looked over his bench and been disappointed with what he'd seen, with what he had to work with. Now he had strength in depth, a number of quality players in every position. Reece James could come on at right-back. Chilwell and Shaw were equally good on the other side. He had Henderson, Rashford, Calvert-Lewin. Now, if the game needed to be changed, he had the players in the squad to do it.

So far in this tournament, England had led in every game and were yet to concede a single goal. But if the team wanted to win the tournament, he knew that at some point, England would have to find a way to come back from behind.

"They've changed their tune from a few weeks back," Steve Holland muttered, as the fans burst into their song about Gareth.

Gareth smiled. He remembered the criticism after England had been held to a goalless draw by arch-rivals Scotland during the group stage. Critics had said that he played boring football, he wasn't adventurous enough, didn't attack enough. They'd said he didn't know how to win a major tournament, that the last few years had been a fluke. Gareth always knew that football fans were a fickle bunch, but it had been shocking to see it so clearly.

In fact, Gareth's choice to play more defensively hadn't been by chance. He'd spent time analysing the tournament-winning teams, France, Spain and Germany – they had won their knockout games 1-0, 2-0. They hadn't been vibrant or attacking. Their success was built on defensive solidity and they were hard to beat. That's what he wanted England to be, and so far in the Euros that's what they'd been.

England started hard and fast. Saka was full of running, Kane was dropping deep and, within the first few minutes, Raheem Sterling had a shot palmed away by Schmeichel.

Gareth shifted uncomfortably in his seat. England were playing well, but he was nervous. They couldn't maintain this for 90 minutes.

Half an hour into the game, Denmark won a free kick on the edge of the box. Mikkel Damsgaard's shot was everything a free kick should be. Hard, swerving and dipping, it whistled past Pickford, for the first goal he'd conceded all tournament. It was the first time England had been behind all tournament.

Gareth stood up and shouted across to his players. "We need a goal before half-time, lads!" Wembley had fallen quiet now and the players could hear him clearly.

"Attack the wing!" he shouted. "Get it to Bukayo! Use his pace!"

England almost got one back instantly. Kane got in behind and scrambled the ball across for Sterling, but his shot was blocked by Schmeichel. A moment later, they struck. Kane fed the ball to Bukayo Saka, who had burst in behind. His low cross was heading towards Raheem Sterling, but Denmark captain Simon Kjær was forced to stick out a leg, diverting it into his own goal. England were level.

In the second half, with Wembley alive once more, it was England doing all the running, all the pressing. Mount, Kane and Grealish all went close, but Denmark held on. It was going to extra time.

Gareth gathered his players around him. "We're 30 minutes from becoming the first England team to reach a final of a tournament in 50 years," he told them. "Three years ago, we slipped up at this stage. We didn't make the final in Russia. Let's make sure we reach it here."

He'd already subbed on Jack Grealish, and now Gareth added Phil Foden and Jordan Henderson – a mix of youth and experience.

Moments before half-time in extra time, England finally broke down the Danish defence. Raheem Sterling twisted and turned his way into the box, before he tumbled under a challenge from a couple of Danish defenders. Penalty!

Gareth punched the air with his fist. With someone as prolific as Kane, that was basically a goal.

He watched from the sidelines as Harry Kane struck

the ball cleanly, putting it to his right. But Schmeichel managed to get a hand to it, pushing it away from goal. It fell straight back at the feet of Kane, who made no mistake the second time. England were ahead in the Euro 2020 semi-final.

Now it was a matter of holding on. Expecting Denmark to find another gear, and looking to see the game out, Gareth threw on defender Kieran Trippier. But Denmark's charge never came. England were confident, assured, passing the ball around as if it was a friendly. This was a team who knew they were going to win. And that's what they did.

England were into the final of a European Championship.

Gareth smiled as the fans started singing "Sweet Caroline", England's unofficial song. The players were celebrating, dancing. He allowed them this moment for now. But, from tomorrow, it would be all business once more. England would be involved on the final day of a tournament for the first time since 1966.

But it wasn't just about getting to the final. Gareth wanted to win.

20
FINALIST

July 2021, Wembley Stadium, London, England
Euro 2020 Final, England v Italy

Three at the back? Or 4-2-3-1? Or 4-3-3? Stick with Rice and Phillips, or bring in the experience of Henderson? Saka on the right, or bring Grealish in? Those were the questions that plagued Gareth before the biggest game of his life – against Italy, in a European Championship final.

Italy had knocked England out of major tournaments

in 2012 and 2014, and they'd been in brilliant form in this tournament – the team to beat. They had a powerful defence, with the old heads of Bonucci and Chiellini in front of one of the best keepers in the world, Gianluigi Donnarumma. In midfield they had Jorginho, Verratti, the skills of Barella, Insigne and Chiesa.

They were exactly the type of team that England had struggled against in the past – teams with class in possession, teams with an ability to keep the ball.

"We want to keep it away from the middle," Gareth said to Steve Holland. "We won't win that battle."

"We've got better midfielders than we had three years ago," Holland replied. "Rice, Phillips, Mount … "

"We play to our strengths," Gareth said. "Wide players, mix it up. We don't want them to know what to expect."

He decided to throw out the 4-3-3 that England had been using all tournament, and return to the 3-4-3 that had guided them so well before.

Kieran Trippier would return to the side, with Walker dropping into centre-back. Bukayo Saka would be on the bench. It was harsh on the youngster, but Gareth knew he would be getting on the pitch at some point. They'd need all their subs to get something out of the game.

Not surprisingly, there was a carnival atmosphere inside Wembley. After all, this was England's first major final in over 50 years – and it was being played on home turf. The pressure was huge.

Gareth had made a big call switching to three-at-the-back, but he was vindicated almost instantly. Kane spread the ball wide for Kieran Trippier, who burst clear, set himself and lifted a cross into the box.

Coming in was the other wing-back, Luke Shaw, who smashed the ball past Donnarumma. England had the lead.

Gareth pumped his fist, but stayed cool. He remembered 2018, when England had taken an early lead, only to be beaten by Croatia. There was a long time left in this game.

Gradually, Italy began to get a foothold back in the game. They were taking the chances.

"Jorginho and Verratti are dictating this," Gareth sighed. "We need to get tighter."

But it wasn't working, and it was no surprise when Italy levelled.

Now it was time for subs. Gareth put Saka and Henderson on and reverted to a 4-3-3. He was hoping that Henderson's experience would give them the foothold they needed in this game.

It stemmed the tide somewhat, and now both teams were getting chances. But it still went to extra time. On went Grealish, as Gareth pushed for a winner.

With a minute or two left until the end of extra time, Gareth gambled. He summoned Marcus Rashford and Jadon Sancho from the bench.

"It's going to pens, lads," he said to them. "You're two of our best. Are you ready to take them?"

The pair exchanged glances and both nodded.

A minute later, they were on the pitch. A minute after that, the final whistle went.

Gareth wondered if he'd made the right call. Should he have given them both a chance to change the game, before pens?

"So we've got the two Harrys, Marcus, Jadon and Bukayo," he said, reading out his penalty-takers.

"Everyone happy?" The players nodded.

"Same as three years ago, lads," he said. "Pick your spot, hit it hard. Don't think about anything else. We're already heroes – you've got nothing to lose."

Italy were up first. Berardi scored. Next it was Harry Kane, England's main man. He'd struggled at this tournament, missing a penalty in the semi-final. Donnarumma looked huge and imposing in the Italy goal.

"Come on, Harry," Gareth whispered to himself.

It was never in any doubt. Kane's penalty was hard and unstoppable. 1-1.

Next up was Andrea Belotti. His penalty was weak and soft, and Pickford blocked it clear. England had the advantage.

"Come on!" Gareth shouted, getting sucked into the emotion of it all.

Harry Maguire walked up next. He blasted into the top corner. 2-1 England.

Bonucci scored for Italy and then it was the first of Gareth's subs, Marcus Rashford.

His penalty sent Donnarumma the wrong way, but it

came back out off the post. Now both teams had missed.

Bernardeschi scored for Italy and next it was Gareth's second sub, Jadon Sancho.

"Please, Jadon," Gareth begged.

All tactics were out the window now. All he could do was pray. The penalty was soft. Donnarumma got himself behind it and parried it clear. Italy led 3-2.

If Jorginho scored the next penalty, Italy were European Champions. Not for the first time, England's hopes rested with Jordan Pickford.

A little stutter from Jorginho – but his penalty was poor and Pickford got it, tipping it onto the post. England had survived!

Bukayo Saka was their final penalty-taker. The teenager who had burst onto the scene at this tournament, the optimistic, fun-loving kid who felt no fear, no pressure, now had the weight of the nation on his shoulders.

He took a breath, ran forward and struck it towards his right. But Donnarumma was there. There was no ripple of the back of the net. Italy had won.

Gareth stood completely still, waiting for some kind

of VAR check, something to save them. But nothing came. Just the celebrations of the Italy players and staff.

He saw Bukayo Saka standing shell-shocked in the middle of it all, and marched straight over to him.

"Bukayo," he said, seeing the tears in his eyes, "come here." He wrapped his arms around the young footballer.

"Trust me, mate. It's going to be OK. I know that more than most people," he said. "You're going to hear some horrible things over the next few weeks. But none of this is on you. You've had a fantastic tournament, been one of our best players."

He paused, choking back his own tears. "We could have won that game well before you came on, well before pens," he continued. "We win as a team, and we lose as a team. So don't you blame yourself for any of this."

He sighed as he continued watching the Italy celebrations.

He was determined that his England team would be back. They had the balance of experience and youth. They had defensive solidity and attacking quality.

There was a World Cup next year. They would be there. And they would go one step further.

21
NEXT STOP QATAR

November 2021, Stadio Olimpico di Serravalle, San Marino
World Cup Qualifier, San Marino v England

It was difficult picking up the players after the disappointment of the final. They had done better than almost every England team in history. But they had lost.

The support of the ever-fickle fans had faded once again, and now every decision was being questioned. Why had he let Saka take a penalty? Why hadn't Rashford and Sancho come on earlier?

That was the way it went with the England job, the way it had always been. Gareth knew he had to bring the fans back on side.

Like all teams, England had to play through the World Cup qualifiers to secure their place at Qatar next Winter. It culminated in tonight's game, away to minnows San Marino. A win would seal England's place in Qatar.

It was also an opportunity for Gareth to test out some more of the players coming through the ranks. That was the beauty of international football – there were always fresh players, new and exciting talents, to try out.

Trent Alexander-Arnold and Jude Bellingham weren't new talents, but they'd barely featured at the Euros. Gareth was keen to integrate them into the squad and see what they could do.

Aaron Ramsdale and Emile Smith-Rowe were two of Arsenal's brightest young talents, and he also had Tammy Abraham, Conor Gallagher and Reece James on the bench.

England had proved over the last few years that they now had a group of players on a level with those of any country in the world. And it was only getting better – these youngsters were only going to improve.

As Gareth had expected, there had been question marks over his place in this. He knew better than anyone that his CV didn't exactly justify his position as England manager. But it wasn't just about the CV.

Gareth understood playing for England, he understood tournament football. And now he had the experience of going all the way to the final. He knew that he had what it took to win one of these. He just needed an opportunity to prove it.

But first, they needed to beat San Marino.

It didn't take long. Harry Maguire headed them in front after six minutes, then an own goal doubled their lead.

Kane then scored four goals, including two penalties, to put England 6-0 up at half-time. It was turning into a rout.

"We don't slacken off, alright guys?" Gareth told them. "We keep going at our intensity."

Many of the players were young and hungry, and all of them sensed an opportunity to get their first goal for England.

In the second half, Emile Smith-Rowe, Tyrone Mings, Tammy Abraham and Bukayo Saka all got one each.

In the end, England scored 10 – for the first time since 1964. It was the most goals they had scored in a qualifying campaign for a tournament.

"I thought we weren't entertaining," Steve Holland laughed, standing alongside Gareth.

"Let's see if we can do it at a tournament," Gareth replied, "when the pressure's on."

He was quietly confident – and with good reason.

He had taken over an England side that hadn't gone beyond the quarter-finals stage of a tournament in 20 years. He had now done that twice. He had a squad of genuinely world-class players – with experience of getting to a final.

He knew that they had the ability to go all the way next year. They could cement their place as England's best-ever team – with Gareth as their best-ever manager. And he was determined to make it happen.

Not bad for the boy from Crawley, who was told he was never going to make it.

HOW MANY HAVE YOU READ?

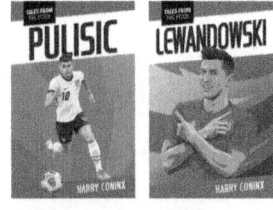

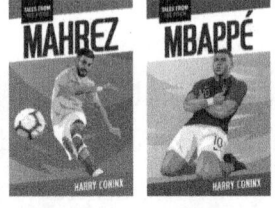

- MESSI
- KANE
- RONALDO
- HAALAND
- SALAH
- PULISIC
- LEWANDOWSKI
- MAHREZ
- MBAPPÉ
- SON
- SAKA
- SANCHO
- FÉLIX
- GNABRY
- STERLING
- RASHFORD
- KANTÉ
- SILVA
- VAN DIJK
- SOUTHGATE
- GUARDIOLA